Mother

And

Philanthropy

Mohammad Ali Aznabi

MOTHER AND PHILANTHROPY
MOHAMMAD ALI AZNABI
2022

Edited by: Mr. Adrian Fisga Luague
Cover Design and Interior layout by: Romeo C. Morales Jr.

Copyright © 2022 Mohammad Ali Aznabi

ISBN 13: 9798842037520

Published by:
M.E Publications
Phase 2, Blk. 57, Lot 28
Celine Homes Subdivision
Bacolod City, 6100 Philippines

DEDICATION

To my most beloved Mother

My mother!
Your compassion opens the door of happiness-nectar!
All the flowers of the world -their fragrance, color,
and comeliness
Are defeated to your love, you are unique, peerless!

My mother!
Your love and affection are like an ocean beyond
border!
Your pure smile and loving face in my remembrance
Awakens in my heart undying divine happiness!
Awakens softness in my eyes, in my heart ecstatic
stream
Arouses the wave of delight in the heart-gleam.

My mother!
I become insane and self-forgetful when thee I
remember!
Under the fringe of your affection, I forget the worldly
pleasure
At your loving touch becomes extinguished my
desire.
You live forever inside me and outer
I wish to lie on your lap at my final departure!
My mother! My mother!

MOHAMMAD ALI AZNABI
Author

PREFACE

Poetry is creation, and its evaluation is carried out from the perspective of a concept of value. The level of creative thinking of the internationally award-winning Bangladeshi poet Mohammad Ali Aznabi gives meaning to the analysis and imposes goals for the appreciation of his work.

'Mother and Philanthropy' is the second volume of verse, after 'Golden Wings of Love' to which I have had access and I am deeply grateful for the English editing technique and the honor of being entrusted with writing this introduction, of an impressionable volume.

His compelling words penetrate the consciousness through images, feelings, creative potential, musicality, patterns, and reflective values of the language. This process makes you live and participate with him, to own the emotion.

Reading his verses, I experienced mystical phenomena, of an internal vibration and intimate resonance, a sum of detours of the human being in search of the absolute. You are a mother, you ara a woman, you are loved, you are son and daughter at the same time! A son, a daughter proud of your origin, of your country, of the nation you belong to. And our joy of being a hymn to life and to the heights we have reached.

Mother is the first source of ecstasy. And it is not by chance that the volume begins with 'Most Gracious Sweet Mother'.

Then you feel how all your organs stir in an unbridled frenzy, how everything trembles in a song, you feel an ecstasy of all the parts of you as in sensory drunkenness when your gaze moves to the muse, the mystery love.

And again, the return to the mother, who is the source of strength always, pure, unconditional love! But the poet does not forget the rest of his family, nor his country! They all have a contribution to make to his artistic meaning and ethic.

We have discovered in this volume, a whole life, an unfolding of destiny, and experiences of pain and love that we have each encountered in our own experiences. And you delight in the anthem of all your organs, in the drunkenness and infinite joy that lifts you in a luminous evolution to your own heights when you read the wonder of his words.

The pattern of thought, and the philosophy of this poet, embodied in the poetic texts is another great indicator of the value of the creative act. Also, the level of inventiveness and imagination expressed through metaphors, comparisons, epithets, and symbols increase the level given by the power of suggestion, and objectivity in the reader's understanding of the texts and is not conferred by the 'impressions' of the literary critic.

Mohammad Ali Aznabi

What do I care about nothingness in the moment of supreme joy, what do I care about death and the vulgarity of existence, when everything is purified on the heights of this dream of joy!

The creativity of the poet Aznabi, is a dimension of consciousness, through successive sublimations, coordinated by the law of harmony and balance, by the law of nature, by the law of love through the generation of a work of art, as a seed, placed in a fertile environment, generates a form of life.

His poems are a high form of education, which is why I propose this book. Life is given to us to sacrifice, to get more out of it than its natural conditions allow. To get more out of life than it can give.

But let us never forget our origins and the philanthropy of this life. It was given to us along with nature and love, other divine gifts as the author writes in his Haiku-rhyme.

The 'Irenic' poet, 'The proud Captain of Mother Bangladesh', wants to see the world loving and peaceful and shows us the right way:
"The whole world is a mother and we are her loving children,
We are bound to each other—all are our dear sisters and brethren."

My dear friend and poet Mohammad Ali Aznabi, writes a beautiful and complete poem. I invite you, dear and respected reader, to discover and open for yourself 'the spiritual door blessed with divine grace', which the poet makes available to the whole world through this volume!

GEORGETA SECELEANU
Romanian Author

FOREWORD

Mohammad Ali Aznabi's powerful verses will touch the core of the hearts of poetry enthusiasts all over the world. His oeuvres immensely speak to our souls. The exceptional talent from Bangladesh shines brightly on his poetic friends not limited to his country but the universe. This south Asian poet roars his magnanimous soul wildly and allows the rivers of his existence to flow uncontrollably whilst it heals fainted and wounded spirits. Readers will be astounded by the abject endowment that this poet grips through his modest inception.

The utmost respect and love for his affectionate mother incomparably melted my depth, being also one. The woman he gives his salutation pierces my heart to cascade with pure and selfless love not only for my belly-born ones but for everyone who looked at me as a mother. His poetry impacted me to the loftiest level that I shed tears relishing his compositions. I adore the spirit working within him that profoundly flickers my edified soul. He is one of the writers I have the best regard for.

HELEN SARITA
Poet and Author
President & CEO, M.E Publications

TABLE OF CONTENTS

Most Gracious Sweet Mother

Mother's embrace is the greatest heaven
Where lies the sweetest bloomed garden.
Where flows the nectar-stream profoundly
That is beyond comparison and felt divine.

The smiling face of my mother is a unique treasure
Where I find my superb spontaneous pleasure.
Her soft soothing eyes can melt me instantly
She is the source of my ecstasy sincerely.

Mother's love is selfless, pure, and quite divine
God's touch I find here -She is my real Shrine.
She never thinks of her pleasure more than me
She is ready to sacrifice all her things for my little
glee.

Mother is the form into which I dive to feel
The Infinite Lord, the Supreme Being with thrill.
None on this earth beneath the sun is so dear
As my most loving, most gracious sweet Mother!

She is my lifelong pleasure, my love, my shelter
Her memories revive me and give me peace nectar.
I have learned to love the whole of mankind from her
She has grown philanthropy in me wider and deeper.

Serene Luster of Nature

M y tears of love and pain motivate me
Y earnings of pure heart create supreme glee.

D ays and nights do revolve with light and darkness
E ndless thirst always leads me towards success.
E ternal desires arouse wave in deep mind
P rofound love in my deep absorption I find.
E cstasy rises in natural feelings
S ource of my imagination in it springs-
T idal waves of muse enkindle my wings.

M ornings, twilights and quiet nights do offer me
O des of rhythmic emotions boundless and free.
T ender feelings bloom fragrantly in verses
I nnocent sweetest words make wave that dances.
V oice of heart personifies in a bright rhyme
A mid sorrows of life rises divine clime.
T ears and sighs create a garden of pure love
I soar with divine wings so far and above.
O n this earth my dreams drink wine from the nature
N othing is so deep and pure as this Preacher
S uperb heaven smiles in its serene lustre.

*Acrostic Poem
*Theme: My Deepest Motivation

Mohammad Ali Aznabi

Montane Spring of Verses

W aves of emotion flow in my whole heart profoundly
H ours of silence pass in meditation on you lovingly.
E ssence of divine fragrance I feel in my depth of mind
N ectar-wine of your love I drink and ecstasy I find.

M oments of absorption fly with the wings of rose
Y earnings overflow the heart and madness grows.

H eavenly pleasure touches my full existence softly
E yes often close to open the door of heart inwardly.
A round me blows the wind carrying your name's smell
R ouses music-wave and enchants me with thrilling spell-
T ears the sensual chains and the passions in me swell.

I mbues my heart your remembrance spontaneously
S erene sky of my mind becomes coloured delightfully.

F low the verses from the ink as montane spring
U pheaval of passion creates a garden-bloomed loving.
L oses the existence of 'Ego' in this cosmic wave
L audable memory is formed in my life eternally grave.

25 February 2022.
(*This poem is dedicated to
Dear esteemed poetess
Helen Sarita, my inspiration)

Let My Tears of Love Shed Forever

Mom! I haven't heard your
Affectionate nectar words for a long time
I don't see your smiling face - the simplicity of the
child.
I get the touch of your affection in the core of my
heart
The sweet sound of your words rings in the inward
ears.

Your manners and speaking patterns flash in my eyes
It is in my thought as if you are alive on this mortal
earth.
You are awake in the pages of memory all day and
night
The showers of affection fall and
Fountains of love flow down to the ground!

I go to your tomb stepping slowly -
I smell your sweet scent
The gentle breeze touches me and
soothes my burnt heart!
The whole heart aches with an unknown pain.
Mom! O, Mom! This sound echoes
just in two trembling lips.

Mohammad Ali Aznabi

The rays of the moon melt and fall -
the flowers spread the scent
The dried leaves fall off -
resounds the tone of melancholy.

The deep sigh of my heart silently blows
In the light-dark midnight
I become mingled in your existence.
Keep me at your feet, Mom!
Throughout my whole life
Let my tears of love shed forever!

Stop War and Let's Love

No war, no arms, no harm, no chaos, no cry, no death
I desire love, peace, dedication, patience, and holy
mirth.
No boast, no anger, no malice, no attack, no bombing
sound
I dream of humility, modesty, sympathy, and mercy
beyond bound.

A little sacrifice, a smiling face, and a soft mind can
stop the war
Self-ego, prestige, and greed, mean interest the
reasons are.
Life is a gift on this earth and every breath is divine
grace
In the cycle of time, all things grow fade, and lose
trace.

Success is here if we can adorn our life with love and
peace
If we can make others smile and create in our hearts
pure bliss.
We all are floating on the wave of time to the eternal
goal
We must reap our harvest in the future -no doubt with
souls.

Let's shake off anger, malice, revenge, boast, and
greed
In the hearts of all, throughout the world, let's kindly
breed
Forgiveness, love, sympathy, fraternity, and equality
widely
Let's make a world peaceful, united, and harmonious
purely.

Let every bud bloom and scatter fragrance around
sweetly
Let the birds twitter in the trees and fly in the open
sky joyously.
Come, smile, shake hands, hug, and love with a warm
heart
Let all chaos, cries, pains, and, shouts from the earth
forever depart.

Great Master Nazrul

O great master Nazrul!
Your memory awakens the upsurging grumble
Of great ocean in my heart.
The warm tears overflow the edges of the eyes
Churning the ribs of the chest
And resounds the melancholic tone of pain.
O, great terrible poet! For what thirst
From childhood, you have wandered
With the restless speed day and night long!

Hundreds of poverties and hardship could never
Stop the way of your chariot
Running like the Kalboishakhi storm.
What an unobstructed love in your bosom
Has risen intensely beyond words,
O, dear! Loving tears fall in remembrance!
None understood your love, your pain
From a distance, only they have seen
The soft scattering beams -
Not have seen the full moon!

The world does not know who is this Nazrul?
What an identity!
Some have seen your creation,
Having not seen the secret heart.
Some being fascinated,
Have loved and praised you.
Some have ignored you of ignorance
Not have seen your light.

Mohammad Ali Aznabi

The glamor of the world couldn't conquer you
You are a great hero! Emperor of Saints!
You are an undaunted great meditator!
The inferiority, the fame-fascination
Could never touch your toes,
Seeing your radiance from afar,
Has escaped in secret.

O Wonder of Creation! Crown of the Poets!
The melody that has played in your flute -
A strange melody -
There rose never such a tender melody
From anybody's chest
I have not seen so much love, so much pain
In anyone's creation!

O silent! O mysterious! O speechless!
You have been burnt by the fire of love -
Like the mournful fragrant incense!
Immersed in Supreme Truth
You, O majestic impassive!
You are incomprehensible! Beyond realization!
It's impossible to judge you!

Only you take my bowing devotion -
The warm tears of my love
The birds of words are very weary!
Stunned is the humble heart.

World Poetry Day
(An acrostic poem)

W ords from pure heart when flow with instinct love spontaneously

O utstanding emotion that overflows self and other hearts profoundly,

R ouses ecstasy in the heart and sensation beyond the decaying mortal body

L audable loving expression from nature exceeding mundane custody

D oor of divine pleasure then opens and flows tidal wave rhythmically.

P eaceful pure dream for the world I cherish heart and soul

O ptimistic people are my fellow friends who are unboastful cool.

E ternal peace is the goal of us overcoming all narrow thoughts

T earing all bindings and chains of superstitions prevailing lots.

R ise up, O dormant hearts! Open the eyes with a positive look

Y onder smiles the nature like heaven- flows unseen divine brook.

D iving into the ocean of beauty and truth, I explore pure love

A midst the creations I build up a palace encircled by the floral grove,

Y outh of poetry, I infuse in me and all beings worldwide above.

Mohammad Ali Aznabi

Glorious Morn of Love

The gloominess of the mind has flown away
In the gentle breeze of love,
Only the scarf of delight sways
With the fragrant touch of blooming petals.

The dark night has fled away
In the scatter of the sharp arrows of the bright sun,
The dormant earth has awoken
With the revealing golden light.

Let the golden morning that is
Dews-wet and sunny with youthful dreams,
Touch the hearts with a soft hand
And let the broken heart rise with charms.

Let patriotism, humanity, and love of nature bloom
In the loveliness of vernal green leaves.
Let the nectar-stream bestrew love-offerings
To the hearts like motherly breasts.

Let the delightful impulse be an unfading flower
In the densely decorated garden of the mind,
Let faith survive eternally like immortal Khizr
In the rotation of moving time.

Let love be ever undecayed like Art
With shrouds of ever-fresh beauty of youth,
The radiant sun smiles in the east -
Let all souls awake carefree in delight.

Sister's Undying Love

Divine feelings, pure like bloomed petals in the bright
morn
Such relation is so frank and cosmic that none can
scorn.
Dawn breeze softness, twilight calmness, and
absorption
Midnight sweetness on moonbeam seems quite a
fascination.

O, my sister! Your love is next to motherly feelings I
trust
Your hand on my head, my shoulder, my back is
soothing just.
Your sweet scolding and the mild dispute is a nice
chemistry
I find in your love and affection -the source of secret
mystery.

Your love is undying, unfading, fresh, immortal, and
lively forever
Because it is beyond meanness of physical sensuous
pleasure.
No curtain of confusion in our love like midday bright
sun
Lovely as dewdrops glittering on the petals - beyond
any pun.

Wish and pray for you for successful happy long life
forever
Your smiling face I love to see always -a wonderful
treasure.

In Anticipation of Golden Days

Trees and plants covered with green leaves
With the dense shadows and birds-chirping
New spring sweetness!

Waves of melody touched by the south-wind
I left behind a tired life
Exhausted body, sad mind.

Yet the bondage is not torn,
It is unbrokenly bound with hearts
We will walk ahead along the road
Treading down all obstacles
With determined confidence in the heart.

Lo! The golden dawn smiles nigh!
The darkness will escape away
The night will end and the dawn will pry
In the heart, pure response of love will sway.

We will build a new life there
With all love and affection twined
Herbs, plants, birds, and various flowers
Will make new arrangements.

Golden life will be our partner
No grief, no mourning in the world,
We will build an immortal life
Pleasurous songs will be played
In the hearts with a sweet note.

Sweetness of Melody

My heart is awakened by the touch of the touchstone
of melody
The maddening vernal wind arouses a response to the
flower garden.
Awakens warm breath in the chest
And glowing lamp in the eyes,
The heart burns as dazzles in dense clouds
The lightning in the sky during the rainy season.

My mystic ears listen to a single melody
Throughout my whole being
And remain absorbed hearing it,
Creates waves in the river of ecstasy.

My Beloved is so far!
At the edge of the distant unmarked realm.
Yet she flows in the waves of life like a fountain.
Super consciousness glitters in mind brightly
Darkness turns into light
With a love of bloomed dawn.

Being lost the sense of 'Ego"
The passionate wave of life-river
Is absorbed in the estuary of love in meditation.
The endless game of glorious beauty
Is going on all over the world,
That beauty hides in the heart of the flower
Smiles in the sky of the evening.

Millions of secret words float
In the face of green blossoms in the trees
With the touch of mystic words
The forests become joyfully thrilled.

The sky and the earth sway day and night
With the touch of a sweet melody
Creates that swinging in the heart of Aznabi
In the rhythm of Universal Unity.

Ode to Myself

I am a lonely indifferent soul
In the middle of the desert sand, I build a fragrant garden.
My bereft empty heart sheds tears
I embrace all pains and sorrows with a smiling face.

Forgiveness is my religion, love is my initiation
The love of the Supreme Lord is the lesson of my life.
My sense of ego has been lost in search of my beloved
The song of separation is played day and night in a crazy drunken tune.

I don't think of my self-interest
I am a calm soul-absorbed in my inner self.
I am in pain, I am deprived, I am heartbroken
The tide of my love flows in the depths of my heart.

I am the eternal lover of the Creator!
I am forever fearless in the midst of infinite great thoughts.
I'm chainless, selfless, whimsical crazy
I am like the irresistible bird -
I soar so high, I am eternally agile.

No one can bind me without love
I want a heart full of tears - I want love and affection.

Mohammad Ali Aznabi

Those who neglect me - throw hatred onto the face
I tolerate all and I travel along my way
with my contentment.

I don't care about sorrow and pain
I tread the death down
I walk along the path of suffering with firm steps.

Tears are my comfort and the touch of divine peace
My heart is the palace of
Supreme Beloved endowed with peacefulness.

Thousands of flower gardens bloom with a smile in
my heart
Countless love springs flow in a rush eagerly.

Eternal joy flows in my body and soul
I am burning in the flame of Infinite love.
I am the only secret heart among thousands of people
None knows my secret - everyone just suspects in
vain.

Sorrow is my companion, pain is my darling
With its touch, my broken heart remains calm.
Who can tolerate the pain with a smile
Only he can see me with his radiant heart.

An Unknown Sojourner

I am an unknown sojourner - a strange tune
Resounds in my heart
An infinite ocean of pains flows in the heart,
Tears in both eyes.

Boundless fascinating memories sway
In the mind all day and night,
Indifferent mind I am going on bearing
Pains of memories in my heart.

Many tender-hearted friends I meet but
They forget after some moments,
Who cares whom! Everyone goes along
Their respective selfish way.

Yet some shadows - some smiling beamy
Faces float in the inward eyes,
The melancholic sweet melodious lyrics
Touch me with faintly flowing peace.

In the crowd of thousands of common folks,
I am a lonely hidden soul
A song of intense deep separation-pain
Is played in the bereft heart.

I don't get anywhere a sympathetic soul
To whom I will unfold my heart's ballad,
Whom I shall show the blood-soaked pages
Opening the wounded burning heart!

The eyes of people are full of selfishness –
Just desire eagerly for own happiness,
Who wants the touchstone of sorrow
To keep inside the heart with earnest care?

Wounded and burnt I am on this earth
Blessed with the gift of pain from Beloved!
The storm of sighs is blowing deeply
In my whole heart always ceaselessly!

I can't express my unspoken words of pangs
I tolerate the pathetic groaning day and night,
If I leave the earth, I'll leave my unfading songs
In the hearts of flowers -in the face of the moon.

A Shelter of Love
(Inspirational Poem)

My poetic words are flying so far widely
Like a Phoenix above the extended sky,
Spreading the golden wings of serene love
Over mortal earth beyond reach so high!

It sings the song of love with a sweet melody
Scatters peace and emotion wide around it,
Spontaneous glee dances with its tune
Flowers bloom with their touch beyond the limit.

If you call it pure and fresh soft love
And shelter it in your heart garden,
Nest of divine peace it will find -no doubt
And will sing melodious song love-laden.

Ever-youthful palace I'll think it for the bird
Royal, loving, unfading, and golden bright,
The muse will exist in your heart forever
And will give you peaceful soothing light.

The night will unveil its love in the starry moon
Vernal wind will blow here all the day long,
In this garden of the heart the bird will sing on
With mind enthralling melody eternal song.

No Hatred, Only Love

Love creates love and hatred breeds hatred
Diamond cuts diamond, love grows kindred.
Anger and boast are the fire of hell- only yields pain
Love extinguishes fire as showers of divine rain.

The heart is formed with love and adorn it nicely
Heartless life is fruitless and passes vainly.
Feel the heart in you with soft melted grace
Find the heaven in you in your smiling face.

Forget the faults, forgive others with greatness
You can win others' hearts and it offers freshness.
Breathe peacefully and look at the earth gratefully
Your life will be blessed with all that you want truly.

Don't show your power and ego to the weaker
Love is a real power that is unfading stronger.
Feel the transitoriness of your physical existence
Eternal realm is before you - be connected with
infiniteness.

If you realize and drink the nectar of the real loving
feelings
All desires and thirsts will be quenched with joyous
swings.
Find no heaven beyond the earth - here is the actual
truth
The mirror is the world -look at it with love and gain
it forth.

Divine Bliss
(Sonnet of William Shakespeare's Pattern)
***Each verse contains 10 syllables**

Come with a smiling face in my memory
Though you are very far off my eye-sight
Flying with spreading wings - golden flowery
My feelings-eyes can see your lovely light.

Your dulcet tone seems to me divine wine
I fail to express my feelings in words,
Your flower face is my real love shrine
To see your face I dare not the sharp swords.

My Love! What attraction I feel to you!
I feel great glee in your recollection,
In my heart the waves of your fragrance flow
I wow at your beauty's fascination.

To edify your love palace I wish
So that I can see you in divine bliss.

Mohammad Ali Aznabi

Bangabandhu
(The Father Of Bengali Nation)

Lofty generous soul, O Bangabandhu!
You gave your life for the country, for the people
You have shed the last drop of blood.

A stream of compassion flows through your vast heart
O, great heart!
Millions of people have responded to your call
At the radiant touch of your thunderbolt-voice
The sleeping countrymen of this Bengali land woke
up in the new consciousness of Bengal.

You have proved in your life that
A hero never cares about the pains and troubles,
So many obstacles you have overcome,
You, the fearless! With irresistible expeditions!
Who dares to stand in the way of your advancement-
O mighty Hero!
Alas! The mountains have broken into the sea!
The stream has flown from hard stone!

What an unrestricted wonderful exuberance
You have spread all around!
The cold blood has grown warm -
Blown at a rapid speed!
You are like the sea - all the people are waves in the
rivers
The drunken waves that have flowed to meet
The estuary of the great ocean!

The sky of Bengal was shrouded with darkness
The people were silent, without protest,
You have brought down the glowing sun
Tearing the curtain of blind night,
You have aroused the courage in our sad
gloomy frustrated hearts!

Anxious fountains have flown in your heart for
 the distressed people
Tears of love and compassion have fallen
overflowing your heart and eyes!
Dear Compassionate Loving friend!
Applauding psalms for you I offer!
The poet humbly bows at your feet!

You have left at the killer's brutal blow
But have left unfading memories in the hearts
With a touch of pathetic pain!
The evil heretic animal who has shot you
Could not understand you and forgot
Your great deeds and immense contributions!

You are not dead, you are still alive
In the bosom of millions of people
You are still alive in the tears of our eyes!
As long as the sky, wind, land, mountains
and rivers of Bengal will exist
The tide of your memories will flow incessantly!

We'll never forget you, O great soul!
We'll carry you in our hearts!
Your inspiration, your consciousness
will flow in our hearts!

I have shed my tears in your remembrance
standing on this mortal bank
Let you be honoured with glory on the golden throne
on that eternal beach!

Sleepless Waiting

O dear freedom!
The whole world sings praises for you
Who doesn't want to get your sweet kiss?
Who doesn't want to feel your noble joy?
Desire for you lies in every particle and phase of the
cosmos
Your constant adoration goes on in the human mind.
O freedom!
O dear freedom!

How many youngsters have jumped for you like flies
How many fresh roses in the garden have fallen for
you,
Just for you, O freedom!
How compassionate mother has mourned the loss of
her child;
How many brides have dedicated the red vermilion of
their sinthis
How many children have taken the pain of their
fathers' grief?
Alas, freedom!
O dear freedom!

Stream of blood has flown on the streets for you
How many tears of heroines have dropped in the
background.
What a horrible death has happened on the way to
Bengal!
How heart-rendering wails,

How touching tears have flowed in the pathetic
stream!
This pain, this heartache - there is no end to it
The song of this pain will play on in the heart
endlessly!
O freedom!
O dear freedom!

Where are you today, dear freedom?
Your honor, your glory today is bent with shame.
In the sky of this country, there is a sad melody in the
air
Deprivation, injustice, and subjugation are not at the
end.
Where people are under the shackles of poverty and
ignorance
Where people are burnt to ashes day and night!
Where women choose the path of suicide for the
responsibility of dowry,
Where golden dreams shatter like glass, frustrated
minds:
Where children do not get the noble touches of
education
How your music plays there
Tell me, how does the air of independent life flow?
O freedom!
O dear freedom!

O freedom of long-cherished dreams!
The day when every man's face will be bright with a
smile,
Every child will spread the fragrance like a flower,
Where women will rise in the light of knowledge,

everyone will wake up
The wall of violence between the rich and the poor
will crumble.
The day when leaders will sacrifice for the love of the
people
The day when the rich will move the dark cloud in the
generous blue-
On that day Your feet will be in the heart of the
country
On that day I will sing your victory song
wholeheartedly.

You come, O freedom!
In the minds of all in the manifestation of love, in the
generous motto
In the advanced glory of self-sacrifice for the
countrymen!
Come as the fountain of non-violence, forgiveness,
compassion and mercy
You come as the love of the Creator - the universal
peaceful touch.
You come down to the human world, come to the
universe
I am waiting for you
Waking for a long time in a dark sleepless night!

Lamp of Faith

It is uncertain where the ship of the heart anchors
I am floating on the wave -aimless, goalless.
People find comfort in the strength of faith
Love is just a name -
Humanity is the essence, unambiguous.

Name, lineage, money, fame, prestige -
Heart-flower doesn't bloom in any of them,
Not spreads the true fragrance of life.

Life is worthy indeed in the abundance of
Knowledge, love, compassion and selflessness.
When your heart is satisfied
You'll find there the real abode of peace.

My every moment is the grace of Infinite-
A unique gift.
Memory-nectar of the great wise figures
Creates a fountain of energy in the heart,
Enkindles the lamp of life
Dispels the darkness of the path.
Far and near merge into One
Plurality disappears
Meets the trace of Supreme Unity.

Repentance

I remorse for the uncontrolled emotion of my youth
I was brilliant in academics and literature sides both.
I dived into an ocean of knowledge of science, religion
Philosophy, geography, literature and was in absorption.

Greatest and supreme works of the world literature
I drank to the lees and my heart's content with nature.
But I fell in love with someone's visual fascinating beauty
I smelt the physical lust and accessed quite an entreaty.

I forgot my wisdom, my duty, my career, and coming future
I lost track and entered into the realm of vain lustre.
I couldn't fulfill my parents' and my teachers' lofty dream
I lost my freedom, my conscience, and my spiritual gleam.

I married her and two children were born as a divine blessing
I was deceived by her face but did not get a soul loving.
I pretend to be happy but I fail to smile with heart
So fresh pleasure and delight from my heart-core depart.

Mohammad Ali Aznabi

I don't blame her but the fault was in my choosing her identity
I pass my life in the saltless company and heartless entity.
For my children's care and safety, I survive and revive once again
God's grace always leads me and I dream the new land to regain.

Infatuating Gloaming

The weary sun is setting in the west spreading
soothing light
Various colours are playing hide and seek in the
clouds bright,
The nature is adorned with solemn and sober peaceful
silence
Birds fly back to the nests with exhausted wings for
quiescence.

The sweet glow of the sun rays is reflected in the
water of the pool
Dazzles the eyes and creates an intriguing scene-
delightful cool,
Blows the gentle breeze swinging the twigs and
leaves softly
A celestial touch I feel in the trees and the sky
spontaneously.

Nature discloses her most tranquil loveliness in this
twilight
Enchanting beauty of light and shade imbues heart
with delight,
With soundless slow steps you have appeared beside
me quietly
I haven't felt your presence for absorbed
contemplation deeply.

You have hummed a sweet melody scattering divine

Mohammad Ali Aznabi

nectar around
I became thrilled and enthralled at your dulcet
engrossing sound.
I turn my face and gaze at you with my unwinking
fascinated eyes
I have felt that the source of all mysteries of love in
your face lies.

Our eyes imbibe the elixir of Khizr in this infatuating
gloaming
Passionate tidal waves rise in the youth-ocean beach-
overflowing.
The tired head of the daylight lies down on the lap of
loving eve
No heaven is sweeter than this moment we
undoubtedly perceive.

Humanism

Listen, all the people of all religions of the world
In the midst of only human love, real religious songs
are echoed.
Religion is not so mean imprisoned in hatred and
malice
It is above all - it exists in the service of all creations.

Relieving others from pain by dedicating self-interest
Driving others' pangs and carrying all sorrows in
mind
It is the real religion that adorns the world with a
blessing
And pours love into the hearts to the tune of sacrifice.

Just going into the mosque or the church or the temple
Worshiping in disguise with a cap or a tiki or cross-
This is not religion, nor the decree of truth
Religion wants the painful afflicted pure soul.

Feeling sadness for others' trouble, to make others
happy
To love people without malicious heart
Adopting the way of dedication,
Giving up lust and luxury
That is the true religion! That's the absolute way.

Not I am Hindu, Buddhist, Christian, Muslim, or Jew
A human being I am and always cry for the poor day
and night.

Forget all kinds of disparities of religions and castes
Eliminate the stains of condemnation, hatred, and
narrowness of the mind.

Raise just a melody - we are human beings
After all, we are relatives close to one another
Giving hearty love, let's share happiness and sorrow,
Uttering the words of human love in our tongues.

The Absolute Lord will rejoice from the unseen
Heaven
Heaven itself will descend upon the dust of the mortal
world.

Firm Oath

Bangladesh
Country of gold-
My favorite homeland
I respectfully kiss the dust off the path!
The land of martyrs, the land of heroes
The variety of mysteries of which beauty is endless.
With birds chirping, surrounded by rivers
Beautiful as green-
Country of flowers,
The land of fruits
Mountaineering,
Mind alluring
Forest and extended field
Wave crossing
Pretty land
Bangladesh!

The land of the poet, the land of poetry
The blood-soaked holy land of the patriots,
Where the wise saints have been born -
 Blessed country!
Bangladesh.

Here the universe opens the door to the unobstructed
beauty
In the light of day, in the darkness of night.
Here, in the heat of summer, the fields shatter, The
earth feels athirst, restless mind
Agitated form of the storm, crazy tune -
 Bhairabi song!

Here the sky is covered with black clouds
Showers heavy rain and fills the rivers and canals
Here is the raft of white clouds floating in the blue
sky
Kashaban on the river-bank -
Swing of crops in the horizons extended field.

Here in the house-to-house cake festival of Nabanna
Filled with laughter-
Fairy tales of the moonlit night - children's noises.
Here is the cold touch, northern wind, fog-cover
The dew on the leaves - the trembling in the chill
Covered with winter sheet.

Here is the arrogance of the southern wind,
The melodious cooing of the cuckoo
The redness of the 'Krishnachura',
The blooming garden, the dawn of soft light!
Here is mthe other's smile, father's affection,
brother's love, sister's grace,
Sweet nectar of moon-beams
Attractive reunion with hearts.

Thousands of years of holy memories
Is the history of this country
Glorious!, the blood-soaked are the millions of
martyrs,
For the language, the great-hearted Salam,
Rafiq, and Barkat have sacrificed their lives
8th Fagun is painted with my brother's blood
Who had this fire of exuberance in their
 bullet-pierced chests
This Memorial of martyrs, built with

Brothers' blood and mothers' tears
Spread unrestrained exuberance
In the hearts through ages to come.
No mourning - no tears -a strong oath in hands
The flame of patriotism in the heart - strong
unwavering desire.
The language of this country, the songs of this land
Are our hope - our soul!
At the door of the world
With erect lofty head
Let the honor of this language be immortal!
Let the glorious flame be burning radiantly
In the foreheads of a Great Time!

Mohammad Ali Aznabi

My Motherland is Unique

My country is the best of all countries
Surrounded by rivers and mountains,
This country is unique.

Green paddy fair is in the fields of my country
The wind sways its mantle - fascinating waves play.
Endless fields full of green grass exceed the horizon
The eyes are soothed and charmed at this fair of
beauty.

How many colorful birds dance on the branches of
trees!
Their chirping breaks the lazy sleep of the night.
Diverse kinds of flowers bloom here day and night
Spread fragrance, fill the heart - despair flees.

Diverse delicious fruits fall on the way to the forest
The sweet fragrance spreads in the air and the minds
faint.
Morning, noon, afternoon, and evening in my country
Open the doors of unlimited varieties of beauties,
friends!

When night comes, the moon and the stars arrange a
happy fair.
With the fairy stories, the yards remain festive.
The diverse land adorned with six seasons
Full of colorful beauty and delight,
It is my Bangladesh, the best in the world.

Verses of Love

I haven't talked to you for a long time
I can't see even with two eyes-
Sometimes I see
The shadow of dreams in my sleep,
One or two words you talk -
Does it quench the thirst?

I see you from afar -
I am overwhelmed with wonder,
What an intense serenity swings
In my whole body and mind!
Tears accumulate in the corners of the eyes –
 Sometimes roll down drenching cheeks.

The fire in the chest is burning -
Is it extinguished in tears?
Your waving open hair - grave serene face
Olive outerwear and walking slowly,
It seems that thousands of kingdoms
Are downtrodden by this wealth
Tell me how to control - this lover's mind?

Lightning flashes at your smiling face
The star's radiance sparkles in the light of the eyes.
Like the petals of a rose is your charming skin
A mighty mountain spring flows in your flying hair.

Different flowers bloom in the garden - belly,
aromatic jasmine,
Kamini, Shiuli, Rose and many more-
The scent of each flower gives different sweetness
Roses bloom with color and fragrance with your
pride!

Who has no wave of love in his chest -
No sweetness in his eyes,
Generosity in mind doesn't play-
No dedication to selfless altruism
One who does not absorb the beauty of nature
How does that person know the secret
Of the color and fragrance of the flower?

A butterfly sits on a flower and then another flower
The lone bird is sitting on the twig
And calling endlessly,
The little bird is dancing with a fickle rhythm -
What dissatisfaction, what pain, what joy
In their souls!
How do we perceive it?

Waving of Departure

The ship is moving carrying passengers
The thirsty eyes of the people
Towards the dancing waves of the sea.
Upsurging of foamy waves
Across the bosom of the ocean.

Breaking through the waves,
Piercing the oscillating sea
The ship is running
Towards its destination -Teknaf.
So far, the ship advances forward
I am gazing backward
With eager anxious vision-
Dreamy Coral Island!

The sound of wailing is resounded
I can hear the melancholic sound
With the ears of the heart!
Gradually the shady gesture
Of the coral island disappears
I feel deep pain in my heart.

The sea-kites fly away
Spreading blusterous wings widely
Their whiteness is full of heavenly charm.
At the distance can be seen
The shadow of the mountains-
Lovely, tranquil, dreamy!

The favorite island shakes wavy hands
With its coconut leaves.

Mohammad Ali Aznabi

Taste of Life

The cadency of the melancholic melody
Resounds in every chest,
Deep sighs of dissatisfaction
Are constantly engulfing people.

I always see tears-shedding gloomy faces,
Running in unrest after illusion
Is the constant companion of this age.

Sky-touching dreams drag someone
Into the blind lane of the labyrinth.
Someone hurries of getting revenge
In emotion to quench the pain of insult.

Someone rushes in the fascination
Of getting the queen of dreams.
Someone lusts for wanton pleasure,
And always bathes in dirty water.

Someone's heart is rendered in negligence,
Impiety, and grudge,
Someone is touchy egotistic
And wants to snatch more than others.

Someone sacrifices silently,
Wiping away tears without protest.
Someone seeks their own interest
With full meanness consciously.

Mysterious are minds and thoughts!
Someone in love is boundless,
Homeless and indifferent,
Someone conquers the impossible with the power of love.
Someone wanders around in the shadows,
Life goes in vain with fruitless work.

The one who overcomes the sorrow
In the midst of own being,
One who knows the secret of tears
Behind joy and mirth.

One who smiles in defeat,
Whose victory is calm and steady,
One who loves whole-heartedly,
And hurts for the greater welfare.

Who chooses emptiness for ownself,
And smiles at the slightest thing,
He is blessed with the taste of nectar
And he realizes the real meaning of life.

Mohammad Ali Aznabi

Eternal Life
*(On the Birthday of the Father of The Bengali Nation
Bangabandhu Sheikh Mujibar Rahman)*

Great auspicious moment!
Today is your Happy Birthday!
O, Father! Today in the soul of Bengal
The happy flute is being played.

Innumerable flower buds have blossomed
In the spring garden today
Bumblebees and bees are all around
Fascinated by the fragrance.

The fragrance spreads in the air
And welcomes you
Pure smile is on the faces of children
I see moonbeams amidst it,
The smile on your face
Quiet intensive!
Quite loving!
Full of sweet nectar!

On the green chest of young leaves
Draws the beauty of your mind
Sacred soul of this universe
Sings your arrival song.

The Best Child of thousands of years
Unextinguished flame in the heart
Of the Bengali nation!
Eternal radiance!

O the source of inspiration!
In the touch of the consciousness of your soul
The rivers and the sea flow boundlessly!

The diverse beauty of your heart,
Affection, love, and tears,
Are scattered with enchanted soul
In the blue color and red-powder game
In the boundless sky.

Everywhere I look today
Portraits of your various forms!
Millions of children draw and
Fascinated and generous teenage artists!
You are the song of praise
In the soul of the poets and the singers.

O Bangabandhu! The flute of my exuberance!
My whole existence is agitated-
All the nerves are overwhelmed.
The soul swings to your tune - wake's up
And the mountain stream
Blows rhythmically so fast!

Your great sky-piercing heart!
The Himalayas bend low in defeat.
Seeing the depth of your love
For the deprived distressed people,
The Pacific Ocean humbly
Acknowledges the bow.

Mohammad Ali Aznabi

Eternally you are flowing
In the middle of the waves of a great time
Your consciousness is immortal.
Awaken the hearts with the touch of your light
In the pure soul of millions of children -
Infuse firm conviction

Happy birthday to You,
O Father of the Nation!
Blossomed is your love in the hearts today!

The flame is eternal, you are the eternal life!
May this nation of yours
Be exalted in the whole world!

Love's Touch At Lonely Night

When darkness descends upon the earth at quiet eve
The evening star peeps, other stars appear gradually
Birds return to their nests with tired wings -colors
leave
The moon uncovers a light, veil of dismal gloom
slowly.

Night jasmine puts off her bodice to spread nectar
fragrance
The wind drinks the wine of spontaneous ecstatic
feelings
I sit by the window absorbed in your loving
remembrance
Around me, the nightingale of bereft heart sadly
sings.

The ocean of my heart's grief swells up in rhythmic
waves
Often overflows the eyes-beach and rolls down the
cheeks
I create a garland of poems with the flowers of heart's
groves
For my distant beloved who prevails in my vision's
peaks.

She stretches her ardent hands to hug me in mingling
love
Whisper my tears, the eyes grow drunken- senses
move.

Mohammad Ali Aznabi

Man Is Incomplete Without Woman

Nature has adorned the generation
With males and females,
None is superior and none is inferior
On importance.

The sky and the earth have
Close connection for balance,
As day and night, light and darkness
Revolve each other.

Man without woman is vacant,
Empty-hearted, frustrated, incomplete
So is the woman too- sans man she is
Alone, friendless, juiceless, and barren.

As the flowers bloom, scatter fragrance
Remain untouched, unsmelt
Unless the flower-lover
Touches them and smells.

A peaceful society can never
Dream of its real position
Without mutual participation
Of man and woman equally.

As with one leg, none can walk
On normal speed without another one.

Seed of Wisdom and Pleasure

Wonderful creation you are, O the woman, my source of Love!
All kinds of beauties, energies and inspirations from you evolve.
Birds sing in the trees in praise of you with instinct delight
Flowers bloom and scatter fragrance and colorful light.
Rivers flow rhythmically, the wind blows with a passionate soft feeling
Clouds float in the sky, the sun, the moon, and stars glitter twinkling
Day and night revolve in the rotation of light and darkness ceaselessly
All mysteries are hidden in the existence of a woman undoubtedly.
Generation by natural law flows forth only for your gracious contribution,
Cycle of creation stops in the whole universe sans your participation.
You are the seed of pleasure, delight, growth, and nurturing as a whole
O woman! I salute you with my spontaneous loving offering heart and soul.

O mother! O sister! O daughter! O life partner! My mysterious Being!
Diverse forms you have on this earth with virtues and beauties charming!

You have colored the whole universe with varieties of

tastes and dream
I find all sources of wisdom and pleasure in your
soothing bright gleam.
Knowledge, wisdom, ability, the greatness of mind,
and sound health make you perfect
Awake! Shake off fear! Be enlightened! Be
courageous! Soar high worthy of respect!
Come forward from sensuous darkness of mean
confusion
You coiled up the society with your bright light,
dedication and loving infusions.

The Shadow of the Nature

In the natural beauty of a forest
Full of fresh green leaves of spring,
Sitting on the chest of cool shade,
Soft-touch of gentle breeze-
Birds chirping in the branches of trees
An extended view of the azure sky,
Flying of a butterfly spreading wings -
The inaudible humming of people at a distance
At quiet noon, a pleasant party is arranged.

In the silence, I float the boat of imagination,
Along the path of horizon drawn by unknown-
I know, there's no end to it,
The swing of light and darkness
Awakens intense joy in the heart.

People who run after only money
I will never find this joy,
This peace will not be obtained
In the sanctuary of the heart
In exchange for everything.
O, busy agile man! Back to this green garden
You will get a touch of heaven!

Saki of silence will pour the wine of pleasure
Filling the cup of your heart,
Every particle of wind will give endless life
To your whole body.

Mohammad Ali Aznabi

It is in this dense bosom of nature
Where man finds true peace,
A magnificent palace worth crore
Can't give this tranquility.

Artificiality only deceives the eye and
Makes the body and soul fall
In the trap of deception.
None will understand this joy -
The real intensity of it
Unless like me
Takes place in the shade of the green garden
In the unfurling soft breeze.

White Holy Sea-gull

The white-colored holy Sea-gull!
You are our companion on the sea-voyage
Towards St. Martin's Island.

You have welcomed us
With your sweet chatter,
Spreading the joy of transparent love with your wide
wings
By pouring the inspiration of your tireless wings into
the heart.

I have stuck fascinated to see you floating on the
waves
In the moving of the ecstatic wings
I'm fascinated
I have seen your holy beauty being speechless and
silent.

On this earth in the chest of the sea
At the swift speed of the ship
In the swings of the saffron waves
I have seen heaven with two eyes,
You have opened the realm of my imagination-
An invisible nectar-treasure of
The sweet beauty of Holy Heaven.

Mohammad Ali Aznabi

O sea-gull, a white gull!
I have fallen in your love.
As the lost sea sailor sees the waving hand
of the green palm from a distance
And quenches his thirst for the eyes of love!
I have seen you
You have poured a memory elixir into my heart.

By crossing the path of thousands of miles once again
I will be waiting anxiously to come to you.
I see a glimpse of your whiteness closing my eyes
I find the most loving feelings in your imagination.
The love that you've bestowed on my heart
Let it remain unfading throughout the life cycle.

Self-forgetfulness and Love

Without entering through the door of death
No one finds the kingdom of love.
That world is eternal, immortal, full of nectar
Which is not acquired by the senses and the physical
feeling.

Just touching the border of gross biological sensation
The taste of death is realized-
And after that, there is a reunion with Holy Soul.

I have torn the outer sheets
I have crossed the sea of tears,
the mountains of fire,
I have trampled the vast expanse of land
High and low full of stones,
I have trodden severe hot sand of the desert
Where I met with the Beloved
Here only the melody of self-forgetfulness floats!
The mystery of one prevails everywhere.

If you want to get this mysterious search
Abandon your ego - at the feet of the great Truth,
Hit the knife in the throat of the will,
And kill the egoistic arrogance,
The will of the two is not here,
Here one adding one result One,
As water and milk are mingled in One.

The Dalliance of Life

Human life on the world stage
Is a faint shadow of a moment,
In an instant, it merges forever
As the writing on water.

The flower that blooms in the morning
Falls in the evening,
Fades and decays in the dust,
Dries its sweet fragrance-
The softness of the petals is very decaying
So is the life- a transitory scene.

If once lost in the divine waves
In the abyss of the unknown-
Who will find it?
Melancholic tune rises
In the beloved's chest
The hidden wailing swells up
Vain wailing!

The rays of the sun, the gentle breeze
And cool water
Can't hold him
He merges with the earth
In the soil.

I listen to the ears -
In the chest of the earth, a song resounds
What a heart-wrenching song!

Man is a helpless doll
In the hands of time.
Rocks the cradle, makes laugh
Brightens the face in dreamy hope-
Arouses new consciousness in the heart
Immediately drags into the abyss of ruin
Great cruel is the dalliance of time!

The sun of life rises brightly
The black shade surrounds the sun before noon
Time eclipses the glowing sun
The sun sets at an inopportune time.

Who can do that?
This is an impossible task of time-
Only time can do that.
People come to this world helplessly
Go away too in the dalliance of time!

To be free from this eternal bondage
When will people be able to?

Mohammad Ali Aznabi

Game of Life

Life runs after the beamy mirage
It doesn't know where its destination is,
Laughing and crying in light and shade
Everything is like an acting trick.

How many dreams surround the heart!
How many come and depart like memories,
Memories are erased like writing on water,
Some memories remain ever unfading.

Faith and love in course of time
Become justified and proved,
Momentary emotion at the touch of burns
Unveils its hollow worthlessness.

Eternal time becomes a spectator
In silence with a gentle smile,
The game of victory and fall runs on
And rushes forward endlessly.

Philosophy of Life

People's hopes and aspirations
Are based on happy dreams
Offer joy for a moment - refresh the soul,
They don't know the future -
Yet keep turning in hope.

The dream kingdom of hope is shattered
Into pieces like brittle glass.
Yet we dream of hope -of a new stimulus
Infusing hope speeds up the path of life.
A whirlwind suddenly blows
In the vernal flowery moments of life,
Destroys the flower garden -
Rouses melancholic tone,

The delightful excited bridal moment
Is filled with sighs and tears
The dense darkness of dead night
Comes down on the night of full moon.

We have to walk along the path of life
With the river of grief in the heart,
Uncertain is the dwelling habitation
Like the elevated bars on the ocean.

Yet there is laughter, song
And soothing words of the heart,
There is love, affection,
There is happiness, caress,

Mohammad Ali Aznabi

There is desire, cherished craving
The path of responsible action-
Exists pure soul, its sacrifice,
There is generous kindness.

Life goes on along the zigzagged
High and low smoothness path,
One who can tread down the miseries
Can dominate over fate.

Love Philosophy

The desire to possess
Gives the tree of love everlasting freshness,
Gross attainment or contentment
Causes premature death of love.

Physical proximity creates
Spiritual distance and aversion!
Complicacy even if found,
Burning even if not found.

But it is better for creative people
To be in physical distance than
Wanton pleasure and lustfulness.

Life philosophy is quite complex,
One finds happiness in sensuousness
On the border of touch,
Someone fond of sorrow
Chooses the chapter on tears in solitude.

Tragedies are more popular and appreciated
Than comedy-dramas in world literature.
Great Time repays his debt-
With love, tears, and a storm of sigh
In the hearts of the people in all ages to come.

Mohammad Ali Aznabi

Lament For the Generation

A terrible wind of misculture
Has devastated the bloomed garden,
The fragrant flowers of real love
In the heart have mournfully fallen.

A piteous sound is resounding around
Evoking the hearts to newly revive,
The loving nightingale is wailing bereft
In the twigs for the roses to survive.

The azure sky of mind has been overcast
With clouds of mean lust and vulgar sense,
In the wide hot sandy desert of age laments
Alone the wisdom enriched pure conscience.

How sadness prevails in the real loving
Realm of fresh reality and flawless truth!
Our body is getting exhausted, weak, spiritless,
Juiceless like barren land without growth.

O Great Soul! Be reborn and incarnated
To save this generation from illusion,
Arouse wisdom and love in the hearts
And the great world for greater vision.

Love at Sleepless Nights

How many sleepless nights for you
I pass in absorption!
Hasnahena's fragrance pours nectar
Into my heart - sad and broken.

The watchful moon pours its rays of wine
Over my eyes and makes me soothed.
Flame of bereavement burns
In the heart of the stars!

They gaze at me with astonished eyes.
In the scent of the air, I find the touch of
That unnamed and unknown beloved,
I lose my 'Self'
The whole existence calls - "Love."

Mohammad Ali Aznabi

Love and Wisdom

I'm athirst of diving into the infinite ocean of love and
wisdom
Where I'll find the source of divine pleasure and
supreme Kingdom.
Nature is the door through which we can have
entrance into it
Modesty and softness of heart are the golden key of it
to meet.
Ego, lust, greed, malice, and anger are the curtains of
darkness
Which create obstacles to go ahead for access in the
true sense.

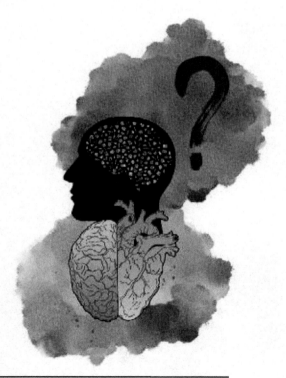

Sweetness of Dream
(Gogyohka)

After so long time I met you in my dream last night
From bloomed body garden, I smelt the perfume
delight
I dived - got absorbed and engulfed with divine light.
Your soft touch gave me spirit in my heart's
gloominess
Woke up from dream-remained the sweetness in
existence.

Immortality of Great Souls
(Couplet)

Great souls never die, rather they enter into the realm
of eternity
They live in our hearts and memories with love and
divinity.

Love Yourself.
(Couplet)

All are in me-and I see myself in everything in nature
So, in loving myself, my lovely feelings around
scatter.

My Dreams

My dreams are like the stars sparkling brightly in the
dark night
Alone I cherish them in my mind hidden but luminous
bright.
Human eyes can see the stars of the external sky in
sight,
But my dreams twinkle in me with my spontaneous
delight.
I love to scatter the beams of my dreams to the world
aright
Which will arouse in sleeping minds the up-soaring
might.

My Passion Won Her
(Cinquain)

I was enchanted at her beauty
My mind grew passionate to offer
Tongue was speechless at her presence
The storm was blowing in my mind
Madness.

I wrote an ode with heart's entreaty
Soaked with passionate sighs and tear
I offered my ode - she received
She smiled to ACQUIESCE as kind
Sweetness!

Gifts from Heart
(Gogyohka/Tanka Poem)

Golden wings of love
May this poetry all you move
To the pleasant heaven
With sweet dreams delight-laden
Gifts from heart to you given.

Supreme Heaven
(Gogyohka/Tanka))

Love and peace to Thee!
My heart melts to sing in glee.
Tears fall down from my eyes
Blow like storm in heart deep sighs,
Here my supreme heaven lies!

Winter Morning
(Gogyohka/Tanka)

The winter morning
Birds in the twigs do not sing,
Dense fog covers all
Across the nature snows fall,
"Come, please, the sunshine"- we call.

Mohammad Ali Aznabi

Patient
(Quote)

I keep myself patient in my creative works through
hardship, poverty and debt dreaming to adorn
my life with colorful love, wisdom, and peaceful
contentment.

Capturing Pinocchio

Lie may bring instant benefit for a short duration but
it yields hundreds of pains.

Literature & The Arts
(Quote)

Literature and the arts are the doors through which
we can enter into the soul of immortality to live in
other hearts with love and emotion through the ages
to come.

Spouse
(Quote)
Spouse is my mirror on which I see the reflection of
my shadow of sadness and pleasure.

A Godzilla Personality
(Quote)

I am true to my heart but sometimes be
Enlarge much by the injustice around me.

Engaging in argumentative stupidity.

Words from wisdom for necessity are golden
Otherwise, better to be in sweet silence laden.

Wish you were here

My waiting days are flying so slowly
When will you appear to me sweetly?
I am athirst to meet you and hug you deeply
My days and nights are passing sadly.
Month of love has stepped at the door
Wish you were here- it is divine or more!

Meditation

I dive into myself and try to know me
There I see the ocean of words and glee
All scriptures and books lie there in a queue.

Ambition

Ambition
Creates inspiration.
Keeps the self in dream
Sleepless passion glittering gleam.
Bloom in the heart muse-buds
Fragrance over muds
Poem-debuts.

Loving Thirst
(Cinquain)

Golden
Land like heaven
Chilly passion grows lust
Come close, O my Love! Hug me just
Slake thirst!

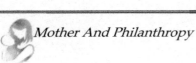

Peace in Love

You are the bright lamp
In the darkness of my heart!
Oh my sweetheart! I want to be your mad
In deep and eternal love.

My heart always calls you
With ardent and eager tone.
My tongue calls with tears in my eyes
With sweet love in every loneliness.

When I call you, I find peace in my heart.

Loving Passion and Vision
Cinquain

Love me
My lyrics-glee
Dive into this ocean
With your loving purest passion
Vision!

Meditation Quote

I am unique unlike others on the common way
I choose my way and adorn my night and day
I am among all but alone absorbed and gay.

Valuing Time
(Quote with 15 Words)

Every moment offers divine gift to me
I adorn it with creative works with glee.

Mountain Valley
(Nonet On Yaks)

Yaks graze in the mountain's plain valley
Snows fall - nature is chilly.
The yaks are callous to frost
Hilly grass is their host
I see the nice scene
Around no din
The sun peeps
Heart leaps
Grips!

A Bunch of Haiku Poems

My Poetry

Golden Wings of Love
Poetry lovers' sweet grove
At its touch minds move.

Mother's Love

Mother's love is true
No doubt inside it does grow
I feel heaven's glow.

Nature

Nature is God's face
I find here heaven's true grace
Wisdom's mystic trace.

Love

Love is divine gift
In purest heart grows its drift
Truly heaven's lift.

Night & Rhyme

Night is the poet's pure time
Creates a dreamy, sweet clime
For writing the sacred rhyme.

Mohammad Ali Aznabi

Value of Literature
(Quote)

Literature refines, beautifies, and dignifies one's taste, attitude
and personality which gives a decent life.

Love for The Distressed

I would like to stretch out my loving, strong hands
To the fallen and distressed of all races and lands,
All the creations beneath the sun are my friends.

Patient
(Quote)

I keep myself patient in my creative works through hardship,
poverty and debt dreaming to adorn my life with colourful love,
wisdom and peaceful contentment.

Mystery of Myself

I dive into myself and try to know me
There I see the ocean of words and glee
All scriptures and books lie there in a queue.

Lament For Myself

I have to endure much with taking pains upon me
I have to embrace gloomy days with tears and sigh
I have stained my life with a wrong decision with
emotion
I have taken baths in polluted and impure water.

I have taken shelter in a snake's hole thinking it safe
I have drunk poison knowingly thinking to be
endured,
I weep and shed my tears in the bereft heart garden
I have offered my heart to a heartless without love.

Constant Star
(Rispetto: 11 Syllables)

Your flowery face with a sweet smile has charmed me
Your wavy figure, rippling hair, lovely skin
Dulcet voice, rhythmic walk, spontaneous glee
Your high taste, simple dress, and wisdom-akin,
All great qualities a pure girl should possess
You have wow with acumen no doubt I guess.
I have fallen in your cosmic love from far
You are my inspiration my constant star.

Mohammad Ali Aznabi

Love And Life
(Sestet)

Love is a divine gift for human life on this mortal
earth
It brightens the heart with the peaceful light of mirth.
The spring adorns the garden with beauty and light
Likewise, love beautifies life with pure divine delight.
Life without love is dull, dim, barren, and truly
fruitless
O, my Beloved! You are my heaven, my peacefulness.

Irenic

(Repetitive poem)

I am an irenic poet
I wow for the pleasure of all.
I love to see others' smiling faces
I am an irenic poet.

I am an irenic poet
I dream to scatter love around the world
I desire to build up a world full of peace
Equal rights for all irrespective of religion, race and color
I expect a loving peaceful earth
I am an irenic poet.

I am an irenic poet
I remain absorbed in a wine of pure love
Supreme love of the spiritual world
Beyond the touch of mortal narrowness.
I lose myself in infinite ecstatic wave
I am an irenic poet.
I wow to see the world loving and peaceful.
I am really an irenic poet.

Mohammad Ali Aznabi

Love Is God Himself
(Gogyoka)

I love all beauty and truth prevailing around me
Nature is the mirror in which the shadow of God I
see.
I float on the wave of muse and divine sweet tone
I suck the nectar of silence in supreme ecstasy alone,
I feel - 'Love is God Himself'- I'm blessed at this
boon.

Triumph of Falsehood

Artificiality and ignorance have captivated
the surroundings
All irrespective of villages, towns, and cities
of the country have plunged into them.
Truth and false, good and evil
Altogether the mixture has filled
the cup of life…

People's day and night
Revolve in the circle of rumor culture,
Nobody opens the chapter of the true sense
Lust-snake spreads its poison
Biting the existence of conscience.

As if anomy has occupied the thoughts
As a virus across the country,
People are moving around
In the shackles of illusion-
They don't get the way of
soothing peacefulness.

In fact, the country is full of adulteration
Bizarre, stupid, and hypocritical people
With the force of money,
leaving justice behind
Have stained the posts of power.

Mohammad Ali Aznabi

Today the sky is surrounded by instrumentalists
With invisible arrogant hands,
So, the message doesn't reach the door of heaven,
And comes back to this mortal earth.

Clean air today is full of pollution-
There is no love or affection in the heart,
Naked shameless mind chases after so -
Seeing the triumph of falsehood.

If you do not understand
The essence of this poem-
And arise conflicts in the mind
Aznabi will sing yet the song of heart
Not looking anywhere with frightened eyes!

In Flowery Land

Cuckoo is sitting in the branch and cooing
The southern wind is blowing ceaselessly,
The flowers are falling in the forest floor
The lover bee is sucking honey silently.

The new leaves are blossoming with dreams
Touching thrill rises up in the garden's bosom,
The swing of red colour arises in Shyamchura
Adolescent buds smile on the mango-boughs.

Lotus and Palas bloom opening the eyes
The bees are humming with emotional vibes,
Tide of love is swaying in my drunken mind
Desire makes me go out in search of beloved.

Where's the beloved adorned in flowery land?
Restless mind moves around to quest her.

Mohammad Ali Aznabi

Fallen Memories

Sweet moments flowing in the wave of time
It seems that they are the dreams of night,
Today they peep into the window of my mind
Harp of lost memory is played in a new tune.

As it were in a remote dense forestland
Papiya is singing with melancholic melody,
The sound of that melody flows in the wind
That grief touches my bereft burnt heart.

Cold wind has come in the memory bower
And dropped all the flowers faded in the dust,
The wave of fragrance-wine doesn't flow
The river filled in Autumn dries up in Winter.

The rhythmic melody that plays in my heart
Is nothing but mournful pathetic and plaintive.

Hope

Hope is the mirage and fascination forever
That gives the speed of living in the world.
The lover spends the night in continuous hope
In the shadow of his reunion to get the bride.

Yet to bloom bud under the fog of winter
Becomes absorbed in hope forgetting the pain,
Blowing soft-sweet wind the Spring appears
Opening eyes widened, it blooms with a smile.

Hope deems to be a puzzle in the dark night
Spreads glow to the bewildered eyes of the traveler.
Life is a boat of hope-everyone wants
To cross the ocean of infinity undiscovered.

Hopeless heart is compared to a leafless tree
Or a heated desert burnt with scorching sun.

Mohammad Ali Aznabi

I Was Reborn

I got myself absorbed in love
Every atom of my body felt
Superb ecstasy of the divine spirit
As it were I had drunk the purest wine.

My outward eyes closed their lids
And opened a secret door to see the eternity.
At first, darkness was there,
After a while a round-shaped light
Rose from the ocean of darkness.

It came close to me and was extended far to make a
way.
From the horizon of the way
An outstanding dazzling figure much brighter than
any source of light
Approached me with magnificent steps.

The closer He came to me,
The more I lost my existence into His beauty!
He stood before me and
greeted me with a compliment.

The surrounding space was illuminated
With the light of His face and
The charming loveliness of two eyes.
I was reborn with my Beloved's beauty and love
I opened my eyes, but I left a paradise
And felt a different one in me!

Great Astronaut

The mind flies to the eternal sky
From one planet to another.
From one solar system to another
From one galaxy to another.

The mind runs at the speed of light
Passing through a great time
It goes to one of the civilizations of the past
Or one of the ruins of the future.

The mystery of human life seems to be fading.
Living a monotonous life in a familiar circle of
people.
Laughter, tears, sensuousness, enjoyment, pain,
separation
Like the feelings of an ignorant child
Great shallow and plain.

At one time I was a great booklover
If someone said, "I have a novel or poetry of
grandfather's time,"
I used to go up to his house.
Going to an unknown, unfamiliar place
I dared to buy books!
Sometimes I would buy books even with fare,
And I would borrow money from a friend to return
home.

Later I became immersed in nature
I was fascinated, lost in the abyss of her beauty.
I collected precious pearls.

Mohammad Ali Aznabi

Then I surrendered myself to the woman
Flowers, fragrances, pains of thorns,
melodies of birds, soothing shade,
Rainy eyes, eastern wind like sighs -
I got a lot.

I want to say in the verse of the Master Poet
"What I have seen, what I have received -
There is no comparison of them."

Then the mind became an astronaut
Breaking the gravity of the earth,
It started to fly to the Infinite sky.
Silence all around,
Soundless, speechless, quiet, and
Impenetrable silence!
Light and darkness!

Words are created soundlessly
Invisible rain falls in love, peace!
Alas! The cosmic rays show me the way.
The impeccable melody of the music floats
Soft melody, perfume of flowers
Keeps me encompassed!

Life Flow

This life is like the flowing waves of the river,
The path is through enduring various troubles.
Often the speed of life is obstructed by the stones of
barrier,
Yet its arrogance, its relentless speed doesn't stop
Rather, it doubles to the beat - and intensifies.

From a distance the murmur of its music is heard
It seems that a magical witch plays the harp with her
skillful hand,
As you approach, you will see the fluttering foamy
waves-
None can see the grief of this foamy wave
Sway of pleasure outside but agony inside.

The eternally athirst heart is insatiable,
The horizon of aspirations is mere imagination here
The last line of which cannot be touched even by
imagination.
How many tears in the eyes and sighs make
something great!
Many stories and tributaries flow in the background.

The pace of this life goes along the craggy path
Somewhere the path of life is full of darkness,
Sometimes it's bright and enlightened.
Here frequently appears the dark night.
The ever-expected here is just a little bit of sunshine-a
little light.

Mohammad Ali Aznabi

The night of sorrow doesn't like to disappear
It seems to be an eternal kingdom,
Though it is mortal and transitory.
It is difficult to say how boastful the sun is!

Day of happiness swifts in the speed of light!
In the blink of an eye, it reaches the edge
The last horizon of the sky.

The evening curtain covers all the light
The lamp of hope is put out by the wind of shadowy
sorrow,
Where so many words merge into sentences in unity
The market function of this life goes on in the fair of
words.

Here is just the emergence of words, the creation of
sound
Sinking into emptiness again!
Where there is no word, no sound, no agility
Life is there in peaceful, deep sleep of eternal bliss,
The speed of life is lost in the sea of death - the last
union.

Flow of Divine Love

Your heart is adorned and enlightened
With the light of the dawn,
It seems that the morning breeze blows
With your loving and soothing touch.

You arouse in the dormant soul
Response of the glowing exuberance,
You play in the lyre of mind
The waves of melodious 'Bhairobi'.

The dark night smiles at your touch
With sacred white luster,
Silent garden wakes up with your love
With an abundance of flowers.

You bring forth glowing rays
In the heart of asleep night,
You create melodious twitter
In the hearts of birds with rhythm.

You create new hope of pleasure
In my broken gloomy heart,
You remove the shadow of frustration
And arouse the flow of divine love.

103

Mohammad Ali Aznabi

The East Wind

I am the restless east wind
My feet are bathed with the water of rain,
I am homeless, the indifferent lost wayfarer
I'm melancholic breath blowing in the bereft heart.
I raise the murmuring sound in the forest
I play Meghmallar's melody in the sky.
I rouse vibes in the body of Shal-Piyal trees
I infuse thrill in TalTamal's mind.
My touch makes the wild Ketoki and Korobi's sweet
smile
I spread sweet fragrance in all directions
Mallika Maloti-forest
Wearing white cloth
Are excited and awaiting
My Kazaria tune gladdens the forests.
I fly the flag of cloud in the sky
Play the bugle of thunder in the north-east corner,
I play the rhythmic tune on the drum
I inflame the lamp of lightning
I am the chainless restless.
On my way, the Kadam spreads the petals
I adorn the nose of the nymph with ornament
The row of Bakul trees spreads the flowers
On my advent-way, a jingling sound is played.

I raise waving ripples in the calm water of the lake
My kisses wake up exciting lotus,
I danced in the white flowery showers
I arouse in jasmine's body thrilling sway.

I am overwhelmed by the fragrant hair
of the young lady
I play a jingling sound in the anklet at the feet
I play in the fringe of the clothes
In the wine of the corset, I am amused.
I drop the olive blossoms in the olive forest
In the Kamranga forest, I tickle,
The buds of guava are thrilled with a shiver
Chalita forest swings with my touch.
Rains' companion I am the east wind
My path is covered with drenched flower-buds
I'm just a fleeting traveler for a short while
I rush indifferently and madly to and fro.
I say goodbye at the end of the rains
In the miserable sigh of fallen wild ketoki.

Mohammad Ali Aznabi

Show the Right Way

Mother Bangladesh is proud of fondling you on her
soft lap
Victorious song resounded and blows in the rhythmic
wind wave.
The southern vernal wind has touched the leaf-
flowerless garden,
And aroused the crimson smile in the eyes of bashful
buds
The fountain of new life has flown in the dead sands
And a new realm has been created with the sprightly
bliss of heaven.

The nation is exhausted from walking along the
wrong way
You, The Captain, O the brave irresistible! Show us
the right way;
O the great! Bring renaissance in the hearts with your
clarion invocation.
Quake this earth and arouse billow in the asleep still
ocean
Make the twilight-sun rise again on the eastern
horizon.
On the green grass of the human mind scatter the
glow of dawn
And sing around the solemn song with a dulcet tone.

Break the elusive sleep of the nation with your light,
O the bright sun!
O the valiant! Beckon us and we, the youth will ahead
advance.
Your glory will enkindle the flame of the heart-lamp
as inspiration.
Bright victory line will smile on the pale fortune at
your touch
The dazzling sun will rise in the dark sky of the
oppressed nation.

Mohammad Ali Aznabi

Unfading Forever

In the fleeting span of transitory life
Some of your memories are with me
Tied together in the peaceful shady nest
A secret love song was sung silently.

There was a dozing thick glare in both eyes
A tidal wave of irresistible emotion,
There was breath- full of lust in the chest
There was exhilaration in the veins.

In the pursuit of life far away
I have departed you indifferently,
Maybe you too with hidden tears
Have forgotten my memories alone.

You might not stand even by the window
With eager waiting eyes for me now,
Today on the way to go to your home
My feet walk no more with ardent desire.

To get you in the depth of my heart
The thorns of depression are painful,
That brings me songs day and night
Sweet melody of melancholic separation.

The garland of pain has been a gift
A priceless treasure of the heart,
In the loving words of my poetry and song
I will keep you bound unfading forever.

Living Sculptural Poem

You are in the book of my life
A living sculptural poem,
You are in my heart-sky
The glowing brightest sun!

In the overflowing flash of your laughter
I can see the enchanting moonbeams,
In every sound of your words
The harp of Orpheus is sounded.

The look in your deer's eyes
The five flower arrows of Love-god
Pierce the heart,
With someone other than you
I don't have time to think alone.

In the fragrant rose garden of memory
You are an evergreen rose,
You are the insane dialogue of a bereft lover
Performed in the theatre of life drama.

Like a tired bird in the evening sky
Find the nest in this empty heart,
Spread the pure light of the morning
In my world of the dead night.

Mohammad Ali Aznabi

Be Covered

O clouds, cover the full moon bloomed with those
sixteen arts
Or else she will raise the waves in the bosom of the
sea.

Adolescent, cover your naked lovely figure,
Your graceful body!
All the secrets of creation are hidden in this enchanted
beauty.

O, teenager! You kindle a gentle fire
In every cell deeply,
You cover yourself, please-
Or the city will be burnt to ashes!

Homes and temples will all become one,
The hot lava of the terrible Vesuvius will erupt!

O, teenager! Be covered!
Save the world.

Shady Oasis

Loving dulcet wind blows
From your blooming garden and touches me,
I feel deeply overwhelmed
With divine pleasure and spontaneous glee.

Zealous mind craves to drink
The nectar from those flowers like the bees,
Arises unbound thirst for a traveler
Weary and exhausted in shady oasis.

Mohammad Ali Aznabi

Nature Is Heaven
(Couplet)

I.
Nature is the real heaven so far I feel and believe
So, let's love nature, save it and peacefully live.

II.
So far we go from a touch of soothing nature
So worse our life will be losing the divine luster.

III.
Trees, herbs, and grasses with soft green leaves
Open the door of wisdom treasure with pure bliss.

IV.
If I get blessed with the impulse of touch from nature
It's more than being an emperor of worldly royal
power.

V.
Under the open azure sky, on the pasture of green
grass
Beside a flowing stream, I find the supreme Godly
touch.

VI.
Leave me amidst the nature, let me drink the nectar
Running after the urban pleasure is worthless and
bitter.

VII.
Nature, O the savior! Make this earth a peaceful heaven
So that our children can breathe deeply in the safest haven.

Mohammad Ali Aznabi

Lines of Love

I.
The pen stops to write about the first stage of a love affair
The heart bursts open in its infinite mystical silence,
Alas, love! Whoever you touch, loses the sense of existence.

II.
O Queen of Beauty! To whom you disclose your sweet veil
He drinks the self-forgetting wine in your incomparable beams
He gets adorned and flows in him undying youthful gleams.

III.
Little food, solitude, sweet thoughts – lovely loving Saki
Thirst in heart, the flame of love- eyes overflowing with warm tears
When I get such a sweet moment, I care no kingly spheres.

Stream of Darkness

Flying afternoon of Winter
The hustle and bustle of the busy city, the cheap noise
around.
Fresh thrilling touches on the unrest mind
The heart-kissing melody of soft music floats
In the gentle wings of the wind.

The stream flows deeply into my breath
Great love touches me - every moment seems like a
divine gift,
Even amid the material world, I get lost in the eternal
waves of thought.

Strange men and women come and go before my eyes
How familiar the stranger seems to be -
Again, the known become unfamiliar too.

Fresh fragrance spreads in the garden of the mind
even amid the noise.
The city is sometimes deemed like a huge forest
With wild beasts roaming free, unmolested,
The two-legged animals do not know the infinite
greatness of human life.

Running after mere sense-gratification
Impaired senses don't give them a comfortable life.

The heart is full of regrets and
Words come to me floating in the wind-
"Can't anyone stop this stream of darkness? "
A Bunch of Loving Verses

Mohammad Ali Aznabi

I.
I saw the freshly blossomed white rose with glittering
petals dews-wet in the winter morn!
I have been fascinated -
A pure delightful thrill has touched my heart!
But the beauty of your freshly bathed figure has faded
all the beauties!

II.
O Queen of beauty! The enriched abundance of your
figure makes it very easy for you to be proud
When you stand before me in a pose with the power
of five-flower-arrows of Love-goddess
A divine fascination prevails in my vision -
I gaze at you with a speechless enchanted look!

III.
I don't want to show the poetic power of the poet,
I don't like to show the variety of metaphorical
rhetoric
I don't run after fame and cheap compliments from
people who never hesitate to forget,
I just want to shed my tears of love in absorption!

IV.
When you are behind my eyes - I don't know why
Your feeling comes so close to my heart.
So sweet feelings touch me
That is beyond my words to describe!

Tune of Dawn

Birds are chirping at the dawn ending night
The heart has risen after breaking the dream!
The breeze is blowing with gentle kisses
Love is oozing from the silent serene sky.

My mind is gloomy sad-
Tears are shedding from the eyes,
The plaintive tune is rising in the heart.
O the Sun of the heart!
The Mercy of the Universe!
I am broken-hearted, a lost wayfarer!

Bless me pouring Your mercy
Into the vessel of the heart!
Play the broken lyre with a new tune!
Bring the morning light in the night of heart
Adorn the empty garden with sweet flowers!

Blow the soft cool wind in the hard heart
Let the melody rise with a gentle tune,
I'll sing the song of your name on this earth!
I'll scatter the fragrance of it
And spread around in the hearts of all!

Mohammad Ali Aznabi

Earnest Ardor

Bestowing people so much love in their hearts
Where are you hiding?
Where is the flute played?
Being intoxicated by your unknown melody
I run desperately in different directions.

It seems so far to be very near
The waves of love flow in the hearts,
You are hidden in tears
Lord of secrets!
You are the wanderer in my heart!

I can see the luster of your form
In every scene, in every sight of day and night,
You are mingled in every face
You take all the gifts of love in secret.

Why so much love you have given me in heart!
Only tears continue to flow in secrecy.
None perceives my intense love for the heart
Only You are the One who is very close to it!

O the King of eternal love! Ever Secret Wanderer!
Where can I find you? Where is the mysterious
Kingdom?
Where is that Whimsical, Self-forgetful,
Ever Self-respectful Most Dignified?
Show me the kingdom of You
And take a loving heart with boundless mercy!

FPB Anniversary
(Acrostic Poem)

F lowery moments are flying with the golden wings of love and fragrance

P resence of so many artists, great souls who scatter beams and essence,

B lows the ecstatic wind around touching all with the hands of exuberance.

A bundance of mirth is flowing spontaneously with fun and hearty laughter

N othing is to cover the rising midday sun and its glowing bright inspiring lustre.

N umerous buds are blossoming with joy at the touch of intense loving delight

I nnocent fun, songs, poems and dance have multiplied its colourful glamours light.

V oice of hearts has engulfed the environment with the rhythmic waves of pleasure

E ndowed the hours are, with unfading and unforgettable fresh memories-treasure.

R eunion of the loving great hearts is really enhancing mutual friendship among all

S uperb emotions and passions have mingled together in this happy anniversary festival.

A dolescence has risen in all bodies and minds with the touch of an artistic great mission,

R osy and loving dreams of Dear Helen Sarita have gracefully woven the imaginary vision

Y outh of the group admins and members is advancing towards goal with true ambition.

Mohammad Ali Aznabi

O The Most Beautiful

I am bereaved, heartbroken!
Sad songs are played in the heart-harp all day and
night long
Inevitably bloodsheds from the wounded heart,
In the depths of my tears, silent is my words.

I love beauty with an intense touch of a loving soul
The joy-water-stream flows in my deepest heart,
My eyes are fascinated by the babyface and the
flowers
Night-moon and the coy young maiden are so lovely!

Life is lost in the fascination of beautiful creation
My feelings become lost at the beckoning of the
Infinite.
'Where I was, where I am - floating in an unknown
current
I forget everything - only pleasure flows in the heart.

O my most beloved! I've been searching for you from
person to person
You have repeatedly dazzled my two eyes
like will-o-the-wisp,
I think you are in it in a beautiful form
After a while, it is proved illusion-
The sad song resounded.

How many ages I am passing in quest of you
From planet to planet -in the mystery of creation!
Where are you, in which mysterious world -
O you incomprehensible!

Though I don't see you, I can feel your love.

In my grief- in my heart your presence
In my delight, in my eyes, I see your luster.
Your consciousness awakens in the feeling of every
organ
The hard heart melts with profound love.

How close you are!
Yet so far you are from me beyond reach!
My thirst knocks at the door of Infinity.
I think you are appearing before my eyes
In the blink of an eye, the desire to see You Awakens
in the heart.

You play with the mind, O the Restless!
Your game -you just understand -
Everything is your mystery.
Please, Dear, O Dearmost!
Show me your form,
Your creation is so beautiful -
How wonderful you are!

This unfit lover of You
Waits for you hopefully,
When will you come to quench my thirst
Oh, my heart!
I make the loving garland daily
With all the flowers of the heart,
Eagerly I am waiting to touch your lotus feet!

Mohammad Ali Aznabi

Self-Immersed Poet

Moonlit night!
Full moon in sixteen arts.
Calm, smooth, luscious soft melted beams!.
Often black clouds floated up, covering her smiling
face like dense black disheveled hair.

Rays of laughter are falling
right through its gap.
Quite a silence is all around!
Sometimes in the distance
The horn of running vehicles is hitting the chest of
silence.

Autumn sky,
Yet the scattered clouds have made the eyes of
flickering stars disappear
The plants are engrossed in silent meditation!

The wind has stopped,
Yet it has spread its calm cool fringe
Across the light-dark nature.

The self-immersed poet is in rumination
Of painful memories on the solitary roof.

Let's Ignite Our Dormant Hearts

Books are the records of words sprung from great
hearts
Books are the silent ocean of knowledge and wisdom-
parts
Books are the symbol of invisible thoughts and deep
mind
Books are the mirror to be reflected the past age
behind.

Books are the garden of love and memories full of
fragrance
Where the knowledge seekers are like bees drinking
the essence,
Books are the shadow of peaceful nature full of
impulse and vibes
Books are the source of light that guides us on the
way to great lives.

Books teach us to be a perfect human being with a
conscience
Books inspire us greatly to be free from the darkness
of ignorance.
Books open the royal door to enter into the realm of
truth and beauty
Books make us aware of our surroundings, and our
diversity of duty.

Mohammad Ali Aznabi

Books connect us with the people of the whole world
so far
Books bind our hearts together and draw the distance
so near.
Books adorn the world with precise feelings and wise
actions
Books make us immortal on the wave of a great time
with dictions.

Books are the hives of sweet love and enchanting
melodious muse
Books are our most loving friends no doubt that
pleasure in us infuse.
Books are more precious to me than abundant royal
treasure
Books are nature and heaven to me beyond mortal
measure.

Books melt our hard hearts, create a fountain of love
and peaceful rhythm
Books illuminate our minds and awaken us from
sleeping fathom.
Books turn the desert into an oasis, a shady peaceful
sweet bower
Books bring spring to our hearts with blossoms and
blooming flowers.

Life is dark, dull, dim, and full of dearth without
inclination with great books
Let's ignite our dormant hearts with the touch of
books leaving all mocks.

Inner Purification

Hunger and thirst close the door of five external senses
But they knock at the door of soul and internal essence.
Leaves fall after being dried and withered in the winter season
But blossom with hope and dream when spring comes on.

Sorrow and tears are a blessing that awakens the conscience
Life is adorned with glory and honor being burnt into ashes.
Physical lust and luxury create darkness in mind-domain
Wisdom grows from miseries and simplicity lies wherein.

Fasting with patience is bitter but fruitful and insure the return
For purification of body and upliftment of mind by turn,
The spiritual door opens with the blessing and divine grace
Where flows quite gently are the nectar wave of eternal peace.

Mohammad Ali Aznabi

Practice of fasting is a sacred bliss for the humankind
That restrains the beastly feelings and soothes the mind
That sanctifies the emotions and sensation graciously
That leads all towards a divine light of Paradise finally.

Ode To Alyona Gohar
(Acrostic Poem)

A mid the stars, you are the full-moon
L ying on the lap of the worldly boon!
Y ou are the rose in the bloomed garden
O f my unseen heart of peaceful heaven!
N est of my poetic fancy is your eyes
A treasure of pleasure wherein lies!

G od has bestowed you boundless beauty
O f wisdom, talent and generosity.
H eaven smiles on your face and eyes
A true heart never dies
R ouses your face in my heart loving sighs!

127   Mohammad Ali Aznabi

Mother And Philanthropy

Mother is the creator, preserver, protector, and
nourisher
Her loving affection is the best and purest in the depth
of nature.
Her patience, dedication, forgiveness, and kindness go
beyond the limit
She is the visible form of the Most Loving God to be
no doubt a little bit.
Mother is the best teacher in all stages of life we pass
Her love builds our life and makes the way to
advance,
She is the truest inspiration, and her smiling words are
strength
She mingles in us subconsciously with our every
breath.

She is the mirror through which I see the whole
universe
Her love has taught me to love all in One though are
diverse,
The whole world is the mother, and we are her loving
children
We are bound together -all are our dear sisters and
brethren.
We are different though in external color, language,
and lifestyle
We all are One in love, sympathy, patience, and hearty
joyous smile.

If we forget all disparities of color, tongue, rituals, and culture
This earth will be a heaven of peace, delight, and caring nurture.
Mother and philanthropy are correlated with loving bondage
Undivided existence I feel in the whole universe with heart's gaze,
In all the creations the Supreme being is reflected to be only One
Our ego separates us from one another- otherwise apart is none.

Mohammad Ali Aznabi

THE AUTHOR

Mohammad Ali Aznabi is a prolific figure in the International literary world. He was born on 8 October 1980 at the village of Harong in Chandina Thana under Comilla District, Bangladesh. His father is Md. Abdur Razzaque & his affectionate mother is Lalmoti Begum.

Poet's educational life was full of achievement, and he attained talent pool scholarships at primary, junior, secondary, and higher secondary levels. He was always first in his classes up to his university level. He came from an insolvent family and his father was an honest, hardworking, and petty farmer. Poverty could not create obstruction on the way of his acquiring knowledge. He started writing poems at the age of 12. His first Bangla poetry 'Prem Aroty' was published in 1998. His second poetry 'Rubaiguchchha' was published in 1999. His first English and Bengali (Bilingual) poetry 'Touch of Supreme Love' was published in 2005 & his second bilingual poetry 'Pertumed Garden' was published in 2008. Then in 2011 his other bilingual poetry 'Agunjhora Fagunbanshi' 'Falgun Flute of Flame' was published in a large volume containing around 250 poems.

His other published poetical works are 'Nirghum Nimognota' (Sleepless Absorption) (2012) 'Rubaiyat and Diwan' (2014), 'Nirontor Piyasha' (Endless Thirst) (2015). Poet Aznabi's recent poetry collection 'Golden Wings of Love ' has been published by McKinley publishing hub of USA which is now available on Amazon. He has achieved above 300 hundred awards and recognition from a lot of International Literary & Poetry Platforms and become popular widely among the global poets. He was inspired and influenced by William Shakespeare, John Keats, William Wordsworth, and more other famous poets of English Literature. The poet Aznabi gets much interest in Persian Literature and specially in Sufism. The great saint and Philosopher Jalaluddin Rumi, the great poet Hafiz have inspired him much. The poet is highly inspired by the non-communal idealism of Lalon Fakir and Kazi Nazrul Islam. In the boyhood, the poet started his literary study with the great poet Nobel Laureate Rabindranath Tagore's 'The Gitanjali' (Song Offerings). He gained graduation with honours in English literature in 2003 and post-graduation in 2004 from Bangladesh National University. His wife Afroza Ali, one daughter- Afrin Jahan Rifah(19), and one son- Minhajul Arefin Rajon(16). The poet is teaching in Ispahani Public School & College, a renowned educational institution as a Senior teacher in English. Spiritualism, love, nature, philosophy of life, patriotism, revolt against injustice, sense of renaissance is depicted with spontaneous words in his poems.

ACKNOWLEDGMENT

Glorious be the most compassionate God above all
And sublime be the Apostles who all of us enthrall,
With their holy light and celestial loving supreme power
Who purifies us with their miraculous gracious shower.

I also owe to the Nature-the crystal mirror of heavenly
God
Through which I can see the beauty and mystery of the
Lord,

I owe to the love of my Parents and the great pure souls
I have been nourished by the nectar from their hearts'
bowls.

I owe to my affectionate sister Ayesha's selfless
dedication
And to my wife Afroza's caring and passionate
sensation,
Both care me much next to my most loving Mother
And inspire me to advance ahead with serene glory so
far!

I owe to the great soul Sree Provat Dey, my adorable
brother
Who loves me deeply and my inner world does nurture.

And all the friends who wish heartily for my glorious
success
Into my open heart's realm who have always smiling
access.
I'm grateful to my well-wishers Umme Salma Mam and
Syeed Sir

Who treat with me softly as their bosom loving dear brother!

I feel gratitude to my dear friend Georgeta Seceleanu, an esteemed poetess
Who thinks of my creation with her lofty wisdom and greatness.

I owe to the exalted poetess Helen Sarita, my great-hearted sister
Who inspires for my poetic career profoundly in global sphere.

I deeply thank the great, gentle, and loving hearted all the members
Of M.E publications-Joan, Ku Ris, Adrian, Jhake -artistic leaders.

I express my gratitude to the global FB friends who enkindle
The wings of my poetic soul that sometimes dwindle,

My love to all readers, beyond nation, tongue, colour and race,
To all loving hearts across the world beyond time and space.

MOHAMMAD ALI AZNABI
Author

Printed in Great Britain
by Amazon